## PRESENTS

# THE DEFINITIVE GUIDE TO
# FORTNITE
## 2025

## A TOTALLY INDEPENDENT PUBLICATION

Written by Naomi Berry
Designed by Chris Dalrymple

PILLAR
BOX
RED

ISBN 978-1-915994-41-7

Images © Epic Games.

# ALL ABOARD THE BATTLE BUS!

Rarely has a game had pop culture in a chokehold like Fortnite has. First published in 2017 by Epic Games, Fortnite's shown no signs of slowing over the years - in fact, it's just gotten bigger, and faster, and become the benchmark for how live service games should be operating in the industry. It's no wonder the game has an average of 2-4 million concurrent players a day. And hey - count us (and you) in that crazy figure.

This book has everything you need to become a Fortnite maestro - from mastering the art of landing with style to wielding the most powerful weapons like a pro, you'll learn it all. You'll be whipping out 90s, switching to optimum loadouts and bunny hopping your way over to LeBron's house like it's nothing (that'll make sense soon, we promise).

So boot up the game with this guide by your side - let's conquer the island and all that awaits upon it together. Get ready to build, battle and outlast the competition. All aboard the battle bus!

# CONTENTS

# GLOSSARY

We're pretty deep into the world of Fortnite now, but Epic isn't even close to being done. With new updates and new content on the regular, there are always new terms and phrases for players to learn - newbies and veterans alike. Do you know how to speak Fortnite?

## 90S:

This building technique is the fastest and most efficient way to get you the high ground advantage (or reach an opponent who has it over you). It's tricky to pull off, but pretty much unmatched.

## BAIT:

Tricking a player into some sort of disadvantageous situation - like leaving a bunch of kill loot out and waiting for someone to stumble across it, unaware you're lying in wait to take them out while they're distracted. Or luring an opponent into a trap you set in a build.

## ADS:

An acronym for 'aim down sight', which is when you zoom in on your shot to increase accuracy.

## BATTLE BUS:

The iconic balloon-lifted vehicle that carries every player from Spawn Island to the Battle Royale island at the start of each map.

## BANDIES:

Slang for bandages.

## BM:

Short for 'bad manners'.

## BIG POT:

Common chat for the Rare Shield Potion.

## BLOOM:

A weapon's bullet spray once it has been fired. The more bloom, the less accurate the shot.

## BUNNY HOP:

A movement technique that allows players to move slightly faster than the default running speed.

## CAMPER:

Also known as a 'bush camper' (to get real location specific), this is a player that spends a lot of the match hiding, observing and just waiting to jump out and kill a passerby who never saw them coming.

## DOWNED:

When a player's HP is low, but they're not eliminated yet. 'Knocked' means the same thing.

## FULL SEND:

A full-out assault.

## HARRY POTTERED:

Real ones remember when Harry Potter had to live under the Dursley's staircase. If you get trapped under a staircase in a build battle, then you got Harry Pottered.

## HOT DROP:

A popular landing spot from the Battle Bus.

## LASERED:

Shooting with pinpoint accuracy.

## LEBRON'S HOUSE:

Any house with a basketball court attached to it.

## LOADOUT:

Your curation of items and weapons you'll find throughout each match.

## MATS:

Short for 'material', i.e. wood, brick or metal.

## MEDS:

Shorthand term for any item that can increase your HP (not your shields - there's a difference!).

## MINIS:

Common chat for the Small Shield Potions.

## NO SCOPE:

If you manage to land a shot with a sniper rifle without the scope, then you've hit a no scope.

## ONE/ONE-SHOT:

This callout indicates that an opponent is one shot away from being eliminated.

## QUICK SCOPE:

Flicking to ADS for a split second to double check your accuracy before pulling the trigger.

## SHIELD POP:

Destroying shields.

## REZ:

Short for 'resurrect', you'll probably hear this screamed into your ear by a knocked teammate as a polite request to be revived.

## TAGGED:

This either means taking a hit or landing a hit, depending on who's saying it (i.e. "I'm tagged!" versus "I just tagged her.").

## TURTLING:

Playing defensively, whether that's building literal turtles or just finding cover to heal or help a teammate.

## VAULTED:

Fortnite is ever expanding, and there's just not enough room for all of the new additions to the game. In order to make space for new things, Epic will put old weapons, items or vehicles into the vault.

## W KEY WARRIOR:

Any player that charges forward instead of considering a tactical retreat is a W Key (i.e., the forward key on PC) Warrior.

# THE STORY SO FAR...

Fortnite has come a long way since its debut, and while some core elements have remained, it's safe to say that the game's no longer the same beast it was way back in its first season. When did you make your first leap off of the battle bus?

# CHAPTER 1

- Island Name: Athena

- Start: October 2017

Okay, so this was technically before the 'chapter' system came into place, but we can pretty much unofficially call all of Season 1 to Season X Chapter 1. This was the OG Fortnite experience - OG weapons, OG vehicles, and the OG island, Apollo. Things were pretty vanilla back then, introducing some of the key seasonal components going forward like the Battle Pass and V-Bucks. It also introduced in-game events, with the very first being The Rocket Launch in June 2018 (Season 4). From there, the in-world story kept escalating, the space time continuum started getting involved (nbd) and it all culminated in the cataclysmic The End event, followed by The Blackout...

**Chapter 1 kicked off the trend of naming islands after figures in Greek mythology.**

- **Athena - goddess of wisdom and war**

- **Apollo - god of archery, twin of Artemis**

- **Artemis - goddess of the hunt, twin of Apollo**

- **Asteria - Titan goddess of falling stars**

- **Helios - the sun god**

# CHAPTER 2

- Island Name: Apollo

- Start: October 2019

**Did you know that Chapter 2 has its own official theme song? It's called Ruckus by Konata Small and Crispin, and was played in-game during the player's very first drop from the Battle Bus onto Apollo island.**

Chapter 2 was the game changer when it came to Fortnite. After the events of the End came a beautiful, shiny new island - Apollo - that was full of big, bountiful bodies of water just waiting to be swam in. This was the first time Epic introduced swimming, as well as the game's fishing mechanics. The island even flooded during Chapter 2: Season 3. Of course, the island aired itself out and the multiverse got involved again, this time resetting things to a primal state in Chapter 2: Season 6. Then there was an alien invasion, the Cube Queen, and another End... and another island...

# THE STORY SO FAR...

Chapter 2 was a landmark Chapter for island dwellers. Wildlife were first introduced to the island in Chapter 2: Season 3, and NPCs were first introduced in Chapter 2: Season 5.

## CHAPTER 3

- Island Name: Artemis
- Start: December 2021

Chapter 3 was the shortest chapter, with only four official seasons.

Ushered in by Dwayne "The Rock" Johnson (sure, why not) as the head of the Foundation, players found themselves on the flipside of Apollo for Chapter 3: Artemis. The island began the chapter covered in snow, but it slowly thawed over the seasons. If we could sum up Chapter 3 in one word, it'd be vibin' (also, coincidentally, the name of Chapter 3: Season 3). The island went through a lot of drama over the last chapters, and Chapter 3 was a chance to kick back, chill a little and enjoy the game without massive cataclysmic events every week or so. Maybe it was too laidback, given that the chapter ended with a mysterious liquid called Chrome enveloping the island while everyone was having a good time.

Chapter 3 was the first time the game ever vaulted all of its available weaponry in favour of a completely new set.

## CHAPTER 4

- Island Name: Asteria
- Start: December 2022

Asteria island was unique in that it was built from fused fragments of other realities, i.e. pieces of Apollo and Artemis. The instability of reality caused Rift Encounters, as well as Reality Augments coming into play for a new spin on the battle royale formula. Players went from riding skyrails in cyberpunk cities to dinosaurs through the prehistoric jungle - to say Chapter 4 had variety would be underselling things here. It also brought Chapter 4: Season OG, a throwback to Chapter 1 (from Season 5 to Season X, to be precise) - but this time, when Athena was sucked into Zero Point's black hole, it led to an escape route to a brand new island...

**Chapter 5 brought back hurdling after it was vaulted for almost a full year.**

**Chapter 2: Season 3 was the shortest season on record, clocking in at just 50 days. On the other end of the spectrum, Chapter 2: Season 1 was the longest, with a whopping 128 days under its belt.**

# CHAPTER 5

- Island Name: Helios
- Start: December 2023

Chapter 5 brought more than a new island to the table. It brought new and improved animations, new wall climbing mechanics, and even new weapon mods. After the arrival of Pandora's Box, this chapter brought Greek mythology to the Battle Royale island, with its very own Mount Olympus and Underworld. Epic kept things fresh by bringing the players from ancient Greece straight to the post-apocalyptic wastelands of Wrecked (Chapter 5: Season 3), with a first-time focus on custom vehicles.

# CORE MODES

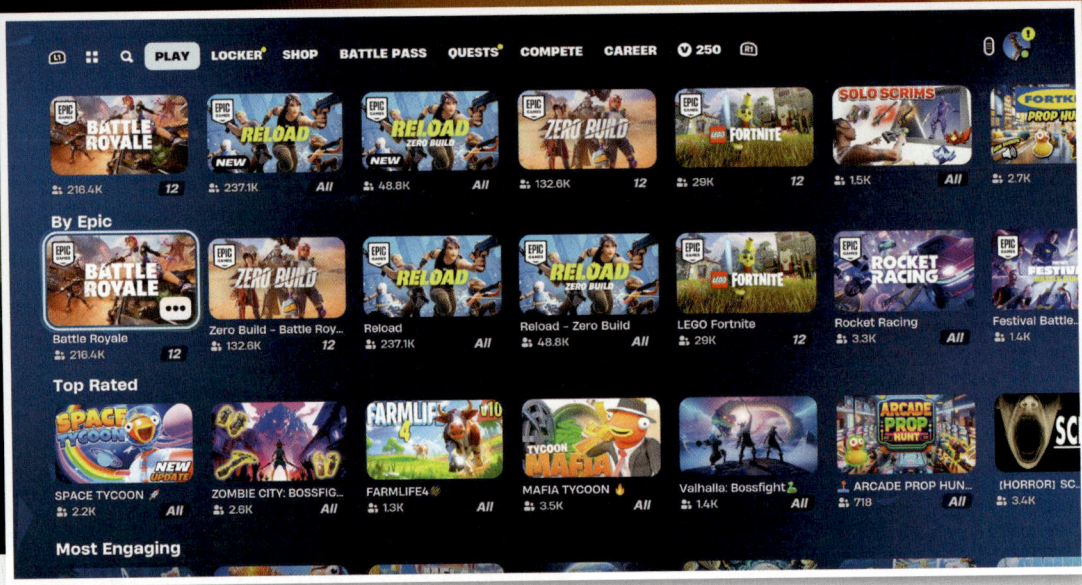

It's crazy to think Battle Royale was once a mere spin-off side mode in the grand scheme of Fortnite. Ah, how things have changed. Now, there are a ton of core gameplay modes that ensure there's always something to tickle your trigger finger when you log in. Where did you join the core mode timeline?

## SAVE THE WORLD

- Introduced: July 2017

This was the initial premise of Fortnite - a survival-based PvE game where players complete missions and progress through a story in hopes of surviving in a post-apocalyptic world ravaged by the purple storm.

## BATTLE ROYALE

- Introduced: September 2017

Save the World may have been the initial idea, but it was Battle Royale that really skyrocketed the game to where it is now.

## TEAM RUMBLE

- Introduced: November 2018

This elimination-based mode has players split into two teams trying to hit the target number of kills first.

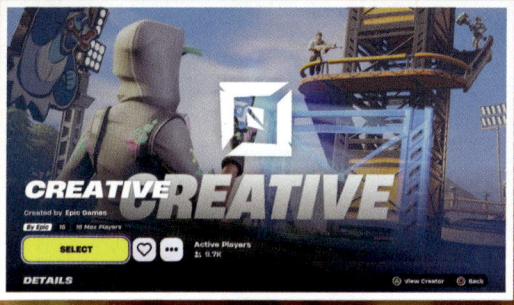

## CREATIVE

- Introduced: December 2018

Create your own modes, your own worlds and your own islands with the best of Fortnite's assets.

## LEGO FORTNITE

- Introduced: December 2023

A survival sandbox where players can make their own village, all with a cute LEGO-skin.

## PARTY ROYALE

- Introduced: April 2020

No PvP, no building - nothing but vibes, baby. It's time to kick back, chill with friends and of course, party.

## ROCKET RACING

- Introduced: December 2023

Rocket Racing is an arcade racer made by the same developers as Rocket League.

## ZERO BUILD

- Introduced: March 2022

Fortnite's build mechanics make it stand out from other battle royales, but let's be real - sometimes we just wanna point and shoot.

## FORTNITE FESTIVAL

- Introduced: December 2023

Time to get rhythmical, as this game has you perform and mix music from your favourite artists.

## RELOAD

- Introduced: June 2024

Battle Royale with a twist: 40 players, squads and duos only, all on a smaller map - fast-paced and action-packed.

# MATS 101

What makes Fortnite stand out from all the other battle royales on the market? Easy! It's the building - a totally unique gameplay mechanic that demands a little more brain power from you in order to develop your survival strategy. So before we dive in to the best builds to survive your 1v1, let's take a closer look at what you're actually building with: mats.

## YOU AND YOUR PICKAXE

The pickaxe is your default weapon, and the only thing you land with when you touch down onto the island from the Battle Bus. It doesn't have much offensive capability, but it's key for harvesting any mats.

### TIP:
Want to get the most efficient harvest? Aim your pickaxe at the target's Critical Point to increase both the harvest speed and mats yield.

# PREPARATION IS KEY

Harvesting is something you should be consistently doing throughout the match - it's always better to be over-prepared and have more mats than you need rather than find yourself on the low-ground against an opponent who's two towers up on you and you've got nothing to catch up to them. The game lets you hold up to x500 of each mat, so it's pretty clear: more is better.

Start looking for mats as soon as you declare your landing spot safe. It's a lot easier gathering mats earlier than later, without worrying about the storm shrinking in and other players snatching up all the resources before you.

Especially as the bubble shrinks, you'll find yourself more likely forced into build battles the smaller ground you and the other players are forced to play in. It's rare for an end-game build to end without a ramp or two, so best be prepared for the worst.

# SO LET'S TALK MATS

The island is full of different features and structures - from neo-futuristic Japan-inspired cities to ancient temples and Mount Olympus itself - but they can all be beat down to the game's three forms of mats: wood, stone and metal.

## WOOD

- **HP: 150**

As the most common mat in the game, you're never likely to be short of this one. It's the fastest to build with, but the trade off is that it's also the weakest. With only 150 HP, it won't take long for any enemy to take down in pursuit (we're talking two swings of a pickaxe, or like 5-6 Assault Rifle shots), and it's also the only mat that's flammable.

The island is brimming with wood resources, like:

- **Trees:** An easy go-to for wood, but be careful to never fully chop down a tree when harvesting. The tree-fall animation is a telltale sign of your location to alert any nearby players.

- **Furniture:** If you find yourself in a residential area, you'll find yourself with enough wood to last the full match.

- **Wooden Structures:** And if you can't find a residential area, you'll definitely come across a fence, shack, pallet... You get the gist.

# STONE

- **HP: 400**

Ah, stone - the middle child of mats. It's both the second strongest and second fastest to build with (or second slowest, if you're a glass half empty kinda person). Due to its relative durability and speed, it's pretty good to use when duelling as it's reliable enough cover for you to take a quick healing break. Stone isn't flammable like wood is, but it can be damaged by flames.

Stone is a little harder to come by than wood, but you'll still be able to find resources like:

- **Rocks:** What are rocks but giant stones? If it's boulders you're after, you'll likely find them near water, like the shore or riverside.

- **Walls:** Again, residential areas are rife with walls for the harvesting. It's best to build up your stone reserves this way from mid-game onwards though; it's a pretty slow process, so it's not advised to do so during the frenzy of post-landing.

- **Stone Structures:** Depending on the seasonal theme, there's a good chance that a couple of POIs are stone. Temples and ruins make great visit to max out your stone quickly.

# METAL

- **HP: 600**

The final boss of mats, so to speak. With 600 HP, it is incontestably the strongest mat available, but wow... it's suuuuuper slow. This massive trade-off means that metal is best suited for pre-emptive defensive building, as it's always a bit of a risk to try to build anything metal mid-duel (you might bolster your chances if you use stone and wood first as cover to try a metal build).

Metal isn't as bountiful as wood or stone, but you'll be able to find it from the following resources:

- **Vehicles:** Don't feel like driving? Vehicles are a great source of metal, but be wary - many of them are fitted with very noisy alarms that give away your position to opponents.

- **Metal Structures:** There's the occasional shipping container and metal fence scattered across the island for you to hack up.

## TIP:
**All three mats can also be found as drops from Chests, Supply Drops and Supply Llamas throughout the game.**

- **POIs:** There's a good chance that at least one of the POIs is a metal-built structure like a factory or dock, so pay a visit if you need to load up (this is an especially quick way if you need to harvest a lot of metal for a Quest).

# PRO BUILDER

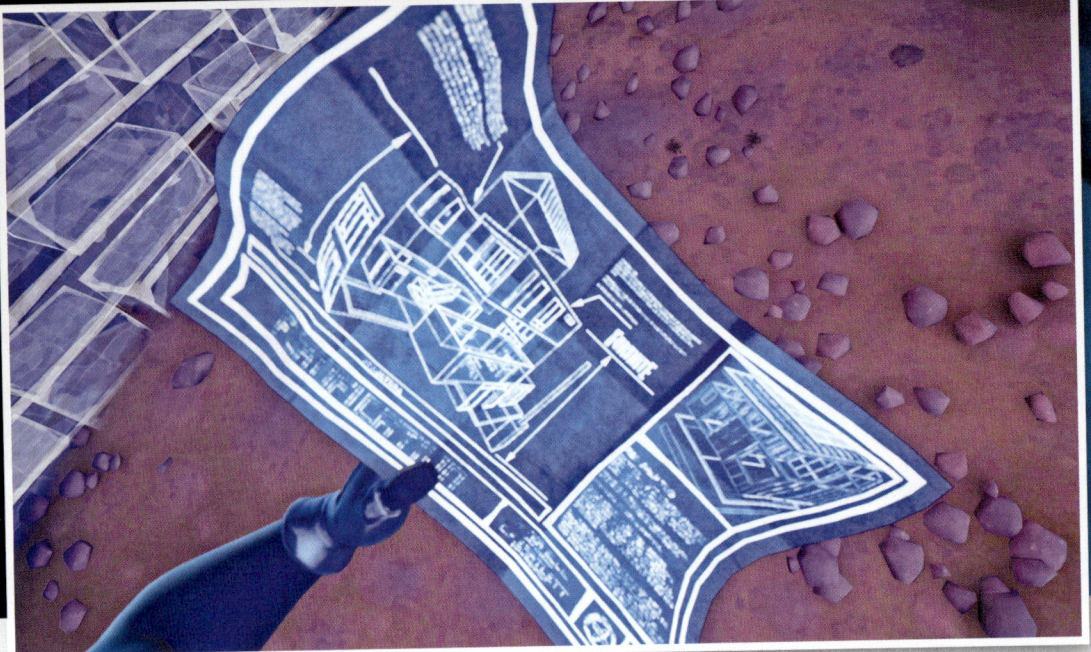

Building is what sets Fortnite apart in the crowded, competitive battle royale genre. It's truly unique, as your path to Victory Royale can be quite literally built over the fallen bodies of your opponents.

While building is essential to Fortnite, mastering it can be tricky. It requires quick fingers, muscle memory, reactive thinking, and a little sprinkle of madness always helps. Whether you're racing skyward to clinch a Victory Royale or leisurely crafting your dream obstacle course in Creative mode, understanding the fundamentals of building is crucial.

But no stress! You don't need to be at pro-player level (throwing up towers, boxing in an enemy in the blink of an eye before jumping from a launchpad and gliding off into the sunset). All you need to do is master the building basics — enough to shift the match in your favour when the game demands it. Escaping the storm, crossing tough terrain and getting the upper hand in duels can all be tipped to your side with some crafty building skills.

## TIP:

Not interested in building or still can't quite get your fingers around some of the trickier builds? Then Zero Build mode is calling your name! Enjoy all the thrills of Battle Royale without any of the pesky building. Hey, we're not all meant to be architects.

# TURBO MODE

Turbo Build is a control setup on PC that allows you to hold down left-click to continuously build where your crosshair is pointed. For console players, the equivalent setup is called Builder Pro. These configurations are specifically tailored to maximise building efficiency. It'll streamline the building process a ton.

**Turbo Building**

Turns turbo building on/off. When on, holding down the build button will automatically continue to build the selected piece when looking around. Turning off will set each building to require one press or click.

OFF

▶ ON

# MATS STATS AND STRUCTURES

Let's look a little deeper at mats and their respective stats.

| Mat | Stucture | Min HP | Max HP | Seconds Until Max HP |
|---|---|---|---|---|
| Wood | Wall | 90 | 150 | 4 |
| | Ramp, Roof, Floor | 84 | 140 | 3.5 |
| Stone | Wall | 99 | 300 | 11.5 |
| | Ramp, Roof, Floor | 93 | 280 | 12 |
| Metal | Wall | 110 | 500 | 24.5 |
| | Ramp, Roof, Floor | 101 | 460 | 22.5 |

All good and well, but what exactly is that structure column all about? Well, I'm glad you asked! You may be able to build whatever magnificent or monstrous creation you can come up with, but there are actually only four base structures you can make in Fortnite:

- **Walls:** A wall serves as your top defensive structure because you can quickly throw it up as a shield when under fire.

- **Ramps:** A mobile structure, the ramp allows you to gain high ground during a 1v1. They're also useful to use if you want to make a cheeky shortcut up to higher parts of the island.

- **Roofs:** This is a more specific structure that is really only whipped out when you need to take cover from above, or if you want to try to box in an opponent during a build fight.

- **Floors:**
Floors are your basic flat structure that are useful for any horizontal travel, like if you're creating your very own custom bridge. They can also be used as a shield for fire from below if you're building upwards during a duel. Oh, and throwing a quick floor beneath you can negate fall damage if you take an unexpected tumble.

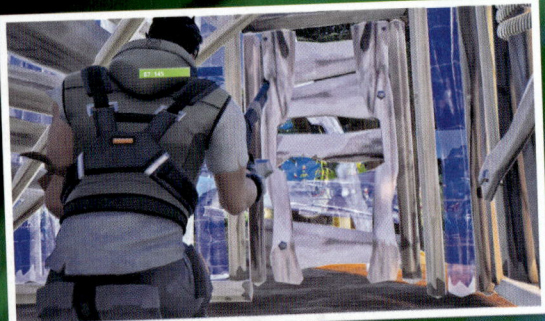

You can also make quick edits to structures. Any good artist knows their masterpiece might need tweaks, and building is no different. Putting a window into a wall can create a great strategic vantage point to shoot from. Adding in a door can make a speedy exit out of nowhere. Throwing down a quick trap can catch your build battle opponent unaware. Keep your build flexible.

# FIRST? FOUNDATIONS.

Every Fortnite build needs some form of foundation, whether it's anchored to the natural landscape or an existing structure. Remembering this is crucial not only when you're constructing but also when dealing with an opponent's build: a solid blow to the foundation can bring the whole structure crashing down.

When building upwards, be sure to build with more than one anchor point - this presents a bunch of targets that your enemy has to take down in order to bring it down, which gives you more time to get onto safe ground and escape.

## TIP:
If you're aiming to take down a foundation, explosive weapons are your best bet. Why waste valuable time (and more importantly, ammo) shooting with another weapon when a single, strategically-placed rocket can get the job done in a flash (or a boom, perhaps?).

## TIP:
Stumbled across a build battle in progress? Protest your lack of invite by striking down their foundations. If the fall damage didn't finish the job, then the element of surprise will undoubtedly give you the upper hand and some quick kills for your count.

# ESSENTIAL BUILDS

In Battle Royale, there are essentially four key builds you'll want to master. Once you've got these down, you'll have the competitive edge in high-pressure match scenarios.

## • TURTLE:

The turtle is your go-to defensive structure, simple yet highly effective for hunkering down. It's basically a 1x1 with an added roof, which might not sound like much, but when you line them up side by side and create pathways through by editing, your enemies will struggle to break through and find you. If you find yourself trapped on low ground with no way to gain the advantage, turtling up is your best bet.

## • 1X1:

The most fundamental build is the 1x1, consisting of four walls with a ramp in the centre for added structural strength. Start by placing the ramp directly beneath your feet, then swiftly spin around to position the walls around it.

## • 90S:

Okay, deep breath. 90s are rough. We know. But they're so good. They involve a series of rapid 90-degree turns to build vertically: ramp, wall, jump and turn, ramp, wall, jump and turn... You get the idea. It takes nimble fingers to nail them perfectly, but with practice it becomes second nature. They're worth mastering because 90s are hands down the quickest way to gain height with solid reinforcement.

## • RAMP RUSH:

For a more secure trip upwards, consider the Ramp Rush technique: while regular ramps get you up, they're vulnerable to being destroyed from below. A Ramp Rush reinforces the ramp with walls built beneath each incline. The stronger version adds a floor, forming a cheese wedge-style triangle.

# SURVIVAL GUIDE: HEALTH + SHIELDS

Fortnite is as much a game of defence as it is offence. If the goal is to be the last man standing (pro tip: it most definitely is) then you're going to have to keep yourself alive in order to outlive the other players on the island. The odds of you making it there without taking a single shot or graze are astronomically low, so you're going to have to know your way around keeping your Health and Shields topped up in order to really master the art of survival.

## TIP:

As of Chapter 5, all legacy healing and shield items have been modified slightly to allow use while moving. This update is huge, as it means no more 'sitting duck' downsides when it comes to a lot of the items. The original items (with the movement lock) are still available in Creative Mode, if you (for some wild, unfathomable reason) miss 'em.

# HEALTH ITEMS

There are always a ton of different ways to heal your health depending on your season, but choosing the right method is as much a strategy as choosing your weapon or build, especially if you're in the heat of a duel. Not all healing methods are made equal, and some trade results for speed (and vice versa), so it's always best to know your stuff about these healing mainstays:

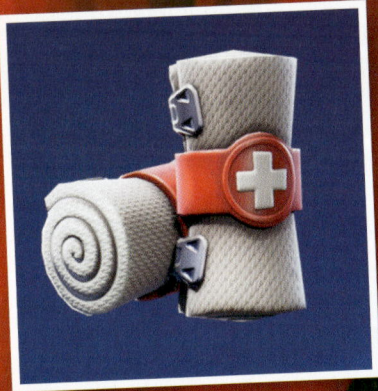

- **Bandage** `Common` : Bandages heal up to 15 HP, with a maximum of 75 HP (or 75% of your total health, if you're playing in a modified game mode). They only take 3.5 seconds to use, so are good for a quick fix. They can also be used as projectile healing, either thrown or shot from a Bandage Bazooka.

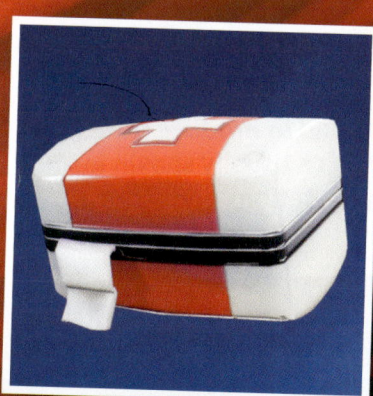

- **Med Kit** `Uncommon` : Med Kits can fully heal your HP, but they take around 10 seconds to be fully used. This drawback makes them a riskier option to use mid-fight, and are definitely best reserved for post-duel healing. If you're taking heavy fire mid-duel and are desperate, you really need to hunker down with some cover before cracking one of these bad boys out.

# SHIELD ITEMS

Shields are absolutely essential fare for any aspiring Fortnite champ. That blue bar absorbs damage and protects your HP, so it's essentially like a second health bar. Securing Shields should always be top priority when landing, and keeping it maintained should remain a priority throughout the match.

- **Small Shield Potion** `Uncommon` : Small Shield Potions (or "Minis") give 25 Shield Points (with a maximum cap of 50). They might not be able to grant a full shield, but they are super speedy to use (just 2 seconds), so there's little risk of popping one mid-battle.

- **Shield Potion** `Rare` : Shield Potions (also known as "Big Pots") are heavier duty, and grant 50 Shield Points (with no maximum cap). They take up to 5 seconds to fully consume, so like Med Kits, they're best saved for when you have good cover.

**Ever wondered what a Shield Potion was like? According to the in-game description, they have a jelly-like texture.**

# FORAGED ITEMS

You can also heal Health and Shields through fruits and vegetables found all across the island. They're not as potent as potions or med kits, sure, but their effects are immediate and their usage time is miniscule, so they're always a good find.

- Apples: Apples heal 5 HP. They can be found in areas with trees (like orchards).

- Bananas: Bananas heal 5 HP. They can be found in warmer biomes (near palm trees).

- Cabbages: Cabbages heal 10 HP. They can be found on farms.

- Coconuts: Coconuts heal 5 HP/Shield. They can be found in tropical biomes (near palm trees).

- Corn: Corn heals 10 HP. It can be found on farms.

- Meat: Meat heals 15HP. Hunting the island's wildlife can yield meat. It can also be used to tame certain wildlife to become your companion.

- Mushrooms: Mushrooms heal 5 Shield. They can be found growing in the shade of forests and swamps.

- Peppers: Peppers heal 5 HP and also grant a bonus 20% speed boost for 60 seconds.

- Slurpshrooms: Slurpshrooms heal 10 HP/Shield. They can be found growing in swamp biomes.

**TIP:**
Foraged items can also be found in Produce Boxes, which usually spawn inside gas stations and stores.

# FISHING

Fish are also another method of healing. Fish are quite similar to foraged items in that they have a very short usage time (about 1 second to consume), but they also are a bit more potent than produce - a lot of fish have stronger healing properties. Check out Survival: Fishing on p. 26-27 for more information.

# PATCH UP SERVICE

There are NPCs dotted across the island that offer a Patch Up service (50 HP) in exchange for Gold Bars. The Characters that offer this service change every season, so it's a good idea to check online to see who's out there on the island while you're playing if you don't have time to do the exploration discovery yourself.

There's also a good chance that you'll come across a Mending Machine on your travels. Mending Machines also offer a Patch Up service in exchange for Gold Bars.

# ENVIRONMENTAL HEALING

The island usually has the odd campsite in the non-residential areas, which usually include a Cozy Campfire. Campfires can heal 50 HP over 25 seconds (so 2 HP per second, if you want to know the nitty gritty) and will extinguish when it's maxed out.

The Fortnite island is always changing (sometimes wholesale, sometimes just parts), so there's a good chance that you'll stumble across a new area or POI that has surprising healing abilities. There have been healing hot springs and lakes full of Slurp Juice in the past - who knows what location lies on the island ready to discover.

# SPECIALISED HEALING

As we well know by now, each season comes with new items and mechanics. Usually, there are season-specific healing items. These can range from regular vault-cyclers like Med Mist and Chug Splash to more unique items, like weapons that heal you when wielding (such as Deadpool's Hand Cannons and the Sideways Scythe).

# SURVIVAL GUIDE: FISHING

Since Chapter 2, fishing has been a major gameplay mechanic that may not necessarily guarantee you victory, but can be a huge boon to getting that final spot if you know your way around the basics. Besides, sometimes it's nice to throw out a line (that's fishing terminology, right?) and chill for a little bit by the water amidst the raging battle to the death surrounding you. Or, you know, a quest is demanding you deliver five fresh floppers ASAP.

## FISHING ESSENTIALS

To fish, you need equipment. The fishing loadout is a bit different from the general Fortnite loadout (though both can include explosives, depending on your level of patience).

- **Fishing Rod** `Common` : They're not difficult to find in the vicinity of fishing spots. You can find rods in barrels nearby, or sometimes even just on the ground.

- **Pro Fishing Rod** `Rare` : This bad boy is a lot rarer to find, but has the chance to hook rarer fish and loot. If your season has the option to upgrade, upgrading from a regular fishing rod is the fastest way to get your hands on one.

- **Harpoon Gun** `Rare` : These short-range weapons can only be used in active fishing spots.

- **Explosives:** No rod? No time? No problem. Just shoot a fishing spot with a rocket for the fastest payout.

All you need now is to find a fishing spot. You can cast a line in any body of water, but if you find an active fishing spot (shown by the bubbling white circle on the surface of the water) then you'll find better spoils.

# CLASSIFYING YOUR CATCH

The fishing game has massively expanded since it first landed in Chapter 2. Fish are consumable, and each type of fish has a different effect on the player.

- **Small Fry Common can heal 25 HP (up to 75 HP). They have a size range of 15-25 cm.**

| Small Fry Variety | Black Small Fry | Blue Small Fry | Light Blue Small Fry | Purple Top Small Fry | Tan Small Fry |
|---|---|---|---|---|---|
| Location | Anywhere (Night) | Coastal | Anywhere | Anywhere | Anywhere |

- **Floppers Uncommon heal 40 HP (up to 100 HP).**

| Flopper Variety | Blue Flopper | Green Flopper | Orange Flopper |
|---|---|---|---|
| Location | Anywhere | | |

- **Stink Floppers Uncommon heal 20 HP. They have a size range of 35-60 cm. They can also be used as a projectile, creating a toxic cloud that deals 5 damage per tick.**

| Stink Flopper Variety | Blue Stink Flopper | Clown Stink Hopper | Purple Stink Hopper |
|---|---|---|---|
| Location | Anywhere | | |

- **Cuddle Fish** `Rare` deal 35 HP damage to any enemy they latch onto. They have a size range of 35-70 cm.

| Cuddle Fish Variety | Cuddle Fish | Blue Cuddle Fish | Green Cuddle Fish | Orange Cuddle Fish | Red Cuddle Fish |
|---|---|---|---|---|---|
| Location | Anywhere | | | | |

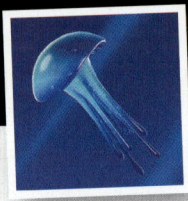

- **Jelly Fish** `Rare` heal 20 HP/Shield to the player it consumes and any surrounding players.

| Jellyfish Variety | Cuddle Jellyfish | Dark Vanguard Jellyfish | Peely Jellyfish* | Purple Jellyfish | Slurp Jellyfish |
|---|---|---|---|---|---|
| Location | Anywhere | Swamps (Night) | Mountains | Coastal | Anywhere |

*Requires a Pro Fishing Rod.

- **Shield Fish** `Rare` heal 5 Shield. They have a size range of 35-65 cm.

| Shield Fish Variety | Black and Blue Shield Fish | Black Striped Shield Fish | Green Shield Fish | Light Blue Shield Fish | Pink Shield Fish* |
|---|---|---|---|---|---|
| Location | Anywhere | Coastal | Forests | Anywhere | Anywhere |

*Requires a Pro Fishing Rod.

- **Spicy Fish** `Rare` heal 15 HP and give a 1 minute speed boost. They have a size range of 30-60 cm.

| Spicy Fish Variety | Drift Spicy Fish | Molten Spicy Fish | Sky Blue Spicy Fish | Southern Spicy Fish | White Spotted Spicy Fish |
|---|---|---|---|---|---|
| Location | Forests | Anywhere | Coastal | Swamps | Mountains |

- **Slurpfish** `Epic` heal 40 HP/Shield. They have a size range of 30-60 cm.

| Slurpfish Variety | Black Slurpfish | Blue Slurpfish | Purple Slurpfish | Yellow Slurpfish | White Slurpfish* |
|---|---|---|---|---|---|
| Location | Coastal (Night) | Anywhere | Mountains | Swamps | Swamps (Night) |

*Requires a Pro Fishing Rod.

- **Hop Floppers** `Epic` heal 25 HP (up to 75 HP). They have a size range of 5-100 cm.

| Hop Flopper Variety | Atlantic Hop Flopper* | Chinhook Hop Flopper | Chum Hop Flopper | Coho Hop Flopper | Drift Hop Flopper |
|---|---|---|---|---|---|
| Location | Mountain | Swamps | Coastal | Forests | Anywhere |

*Requires a Pro Fishing Rod.

# SURVIVAL GUIDE: WILDLIFE

The island is teeming with life, and sometimes you'll find it isn't just the other 99 players out there trying to take you out. Wildlife were first introduced in Chapter 2, and have been keeping players company down on the island ever since.

## THE MAINSTAYS

Wildlife are treated no differently than other items, vehicles and weaponry in Fortnite - the devs won't hesitate to introduce a new critter one season and then chuck it in the vault the next. Sometimes the island will be brimming with boars and wolves, and sometimes it'll be alien parasites and zombie chickens. It's impossible to cover every animal that's graced the island, but there are a bunch of usual suspects that get cycled in and out of the vault.

### CHICKEN

- Type: Neutral
- HP: 60

Chickens are neutral, but they'll attack you if you provoke them. If you grab one of them, you can hold it above your head for a higher jump and slower fall.

## FROG

- Type: Passive
- HP: 60

Frogs will flee when attacked, and their speed makes them pretty tricky to chase down and kill.

**TIP:**
Want to recruit a four-legged friend to help you out on the island? You can tame hostile wildlife like wolves and boars to join you by using meat.

## WOLF

- Type: Hostile
- HP: 250

Wolves are interesting because they can be tamed, which means players can ride them and also have them aid in battle. They usually spawn in packs of three or more, so be prepared for a difficult fight if you want to try to claim one.

## BOAR

- Type: Hostile
- HP: 120

Boars may have less HP than wolves, but you should still be wary of them - their charges can hit real hard if you're caught on the wrong end of one. Unlike a lot of other hostile animals, boars will flee after being initially attacked, so you'll have to chase one down if you want to finish the job or tame it.

**TIP:**
Supply Llamas are unique in that they have two very distinct forms. Sometimes Supply Llamas roam the island like any other animal. They can also appear as totally stationary piñatas. Regardless of their sentience (do you think Supply Llamas dream?), they'll always hold a bounty of treasures for you if you find one and manage to take it down.

# FRIENDS AND FOES

You're never alone on the island unless you clutch that Victory Royale, and it's more than just the other players out there. Since Chapter 2, Characters (also known as NPCs) have been present on the island to offer a helping hand... or aim for your head. You know, either or.

**TIP:**
Want to find out more about why certain Characters are on the island? Take on Story Quests to learn about the game's current chapter and story.

**TIP:**
You'll know you're close to a Character when you spot a little speech bubble icon on your map.

# CHARACTER INTERACTIONS

Each Character has different interaction possibilities. Like all aspects of Fortnite, some of these interactions cycle their way in and out of the Vault, and new options could also be added, but this is the general array of options you'll be presented with:

- **Duel:** Defeat them in a duel to earn their weapon.

- **Hire:** Recruit the character to fight beside you.

- **Patch Up:** Recover a small amount of health.

- **Prop Disguise:** Turns you into a prop for sneaky behaviour.

- **Rift:** Open a rift in the sky to glide to a new location.

- **Upgrade:** Upgrade your currently equipped weapon.

- **Weapon:** Purchase a weapon.

- **Heavy Specialist:** They'll up the firepower with cluster bombs.

- **Medic Specialist:** They'll keep an eye on your HP.

- **Scout Specialist:** They'll scout the area every now and then and ping nearby chests and enemies.

- **Supply Specialist:** They'll drop resources (like ammo, mats and heals) for you.

Each Character spawns at their specific location every match. If another player gets to a Character before you do, you'll still have a chance to interact with them in a ghostly form if they've been eliminated.

Box 3: How well do you know your Fortnite history? The very first Character was Bandolette, the jungle predator in Chapter 2, Season 5.

# GOLD TALKS

If you want to interact with a Character, you're going to need to cough up some Bars. Bars can be acquired either by eliminating opponents (NPCs and other players), or finding some in chests, safes and cash registers. You can also earn bars by completing bounties - you can locate Bounty Boards by the weapon scope symbol on your map.

## TIP:
Looking to hire a Character? Each hireable NPC is a specific Specialist, which affects how they can help you during the match.

## TIP:
Cracking a safe for some Bars? Be wary of your surroundings - opening safes have an audio cue that could give away your location to nearby enemies.

# KNOW YOUR ARSENAL

Building and fishing and whatnot are all fun and games, but the basis of Fortnite is gunplay. As soon as you touch down on the island from the Battle Bus, there's the risk of getting sniped out by an opponent (or even an aggro NPC, since they're packing now too). Sure, you can do your best to pull off a pacifist run and try to let everyone else deal with each other, but if you want to snatch that Victory Royale within the final Storm bubble, you're going to need to wield a weapon or two.

With an ever-changing arsenal, Fortnite always has a new toy for you to play with, but every pro worth their salt knows their way around the basics of the Fortnite weapon roster.

## AMMO

Any form of ranged weaponry requires ammo, but each weapon type needs a specific ammo type. Ammo has a variety of ranges (close to long) and damage per shot (also known as DPS).

Ammo can be found in chests, ammo boxes, supply boxes, and also just on the ground. When it comes to ammo, the more the merrier - just stack as much as you can, because you're always better to have more than the occasion calls for than less (and don't learn that the hard way).

| Ammo Type | Weapon Type | Effective Range | Damage Per Shot |
|---|---|---|---|
| Light Ammo | Pistols, SMGs | Close | Low |
| Medium Ammo | Pistols, Assault Rifles | Mid | Medium |
| Heavy Ammo | Sniper Rifles | Long | High |
| Shells | Shotguns | Close | High |
| Arrows | Bows, Crossbows | Mid | Low |
| Rockets | Explosives | Mid/Long | Very High |

# RARITIES

The rarity hierarchy is a base system that pretty much every item in Fortnite falls under. The general rule of thumb is the rarer the better - but if we want to get weapon-specific, a weapon's rarity indicates its firepower, its reload time and its chances of being found during a match.

**Common < Uncommon < Rare < Epic < Legendary < Mythic < Exotic**

Mythic and Exotic weapons cannot be found on the map. You're going to have to duel an NPC to get your hands on a Mythic, or cough up some Bars to exchange for an Exotic. For more information about weapons from NPCs, check out the Friends and Foes chapter on p. 30-31.

## TIP:
Pro tip! When it comes to thinking about rarity, it's a good idea to consider it in the context of weapon type. A Legendary Pistol is always going to be better than a Common Pistol, but it's not necessarily better than an Uncommon Shotgun, depending on the situation. A well balanced loadout prioritises weapon type and variety over rarity.

# UPGRADING WEAPONS

You don't have to be stuck with a bunch of Common duds if you know where to look. Weapon upgrading was first introduced back in Chapter 2, and modding was introduced in Chapter 5. While the methods differ, the outcome is the same: making a more deadly weapon out of the existing one.

Usually the methods of doing so are mutually exclusive. Epic switches between upgrading methods and modding depending on the season, so be sure to check out which is active before hunting one of them down on the island:

- **UPGRADE BENCHES:**
  Located across the island, but more commonly found in POIs and named locations.

- **NPCS:**
  Some of the friendly NPCs are happy to exchange Bars to upgrade a weapon.

- **MOD BENCHES:**
  Mod benches can change a weapon's mod (optic, magazine, underbarrel or barrel).

All three methods require Bars. Mod benches charge 75 Bars to equip a mod. Upgrading affects the weapon's rarity, so the cost depends on the rarity level.

| Rarity Upgrade | Cost (Bars) |
|---|---|
| Common → Uncommon | 200 |
| Uncommon → Rare | 300 |
| Rare → Epic | 400 |
| Epic → Legendary | 500 |

# WEAPON TYPES

So we've covered weapon rarity, and we've covered weapon upgrading/modding... Now it's time to dive into the meat of the matter: weapon types. There have been some real outlandish weapons in Fortnite over the years, but regardless of how weird the arsenal gets, it always boils down to the same categories of weapon type that the game established from its very start.

## BOWS AND CROSSBOWS

This weapon type often finds itself frequently vaulted, but there's a good chance a variation will make its way into circulation when a season changes (especially if it's a themed season). As a projectile weapon, they require predictive tracking in order to hit their target.

- Due to their lower damage output, they're not effective weapons to demolish any structures or tackle tougher enemy NPCs.

- Bows utilise targeting arcs similar to throwable items.

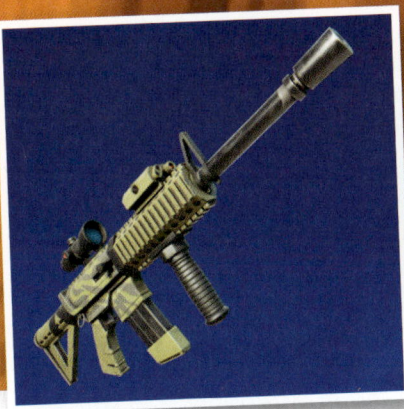

## ASSAULT RIFLES

These guns are well balanced as they're effective mid to long range and have a high damage output. Having a medium to high capacity magazine also allows fast and heavy gunfire.

- The primary weakness of the assault rifle is undoubtedly its bloom. To get around this, it's best to capitalise on its first shot accuracy by aiming for a headshot initially, then adjust your aim to target the body to manage the bloom effectively.

- Assault rifles experience damage drop-off starting at about 50 metres, reducing gradually to a minimum damage output of 66%.

## EXPLOSIVES

Explosive weapons are projectiles, which means they require predictive tracking. They're pretty slow to fire, but pack a real punch when they land - this means they're best suited for bigger targets like vehicles or structures.

- Due to splash damage, using an explosive weapon up close means you risk taking friendly fire.

- Need to bring down a structure quickly? A well-placed explosive at the foundation will get the job done swiftly.

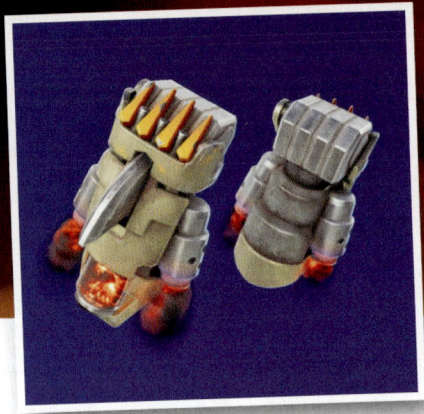

# MELEE

Melee weapons don't require any ammo, which means they're strictly for close range usage only (and real close, at that). Your pickaxe is technically a melee weapon, though it doesn't do a lot of real damage. Many of the game's collaboration weapons fall into this category, like Michaelangelo's Nunchaku, the Kingsman umbrella or the Star Wars lightsabers.

# PISTOLS

Pistols are kind of middle of the pack, but they ultimately get the job done and are never a bad option to have. Sure, if you have the option of another weapon type, go ahead and drop your pistol - but don't deliberately skip over one if you've got space in your loadout. The pistol is good for close to mid range.

- If you want to make the most of a pistol, pair it with a rifle or an SMG.

- Pistols that use Light Ammo have great hip fire accuracy.

# SHOTGUNS

Shotguns are the weapon of choice for any player that's serious about their duelling. They're crazy effective in close range, with a high DPS and forgiving area of effect. But their insane strength close up comes at the cost of being pretty useless at any other range.

- Waiting for your shotgun to reload can make or break a duel. A useful tip to speed up shotgun reload times is to keep your ammo topped up regularly. Partial reloads are quicker than full ones, allowing you to maintain a faster pace in combat.

- Shotguns are an absolute must if you want to get that Victory Royale. You should always prioritise getting your hands on one for your loadout ASAP.

## SNIPER RIFLES

The weapon of choice for long range assassins. Sniper rifles deal significant damage at long distance. These can be tricky for newbies to handle, as their effectiveness relies fully on its wielder's ability to aim and track their target.

- Sniper rifles are perfectly paired with close range weaponry. It's always best to be prepared to make a quick switch to something close range if your sniping session is interrupted.

- Trying to get better at tracking? Aim ahead of the target instead of at them directly. Aiming ahead considers bullet speed and drop.

## SUBMACHINE GUNS (SMGS)

SMGs are the GOAT when it comes to close range combat - they just can't be beat. Their DPS is super high but very range dependent; with high damage drop off and bullet spray, they're pretty much ineffectual from any further than mid range.

- SMGs go great with pistols, or any other gun that has a decent mid range. Use another gun to close the distance, and then switch to the SMG up close.

- SMGs can eat their way through a lot of ammo without you realising, so try to use short and controlled bursts when firing to stay on top of that.

## TRAPS

Trap weapons are all about being proactive and defensive in combat. Drop them to fortify your position or catch opponents off guard during intense build battles.

# DUEL MAESTRO

Whether you're diving down onto the island with a high kill count at the top of your priority list, or hoping the only battle you'll need to take part in is the final 1v1 for the crown, mastering the art of the duel is an absolute must to secure the Victory Royale.

## KEEP YOUR LOADOUT PREPARED

Who knows what's awaiting you around the corner? It could be another player, or even a blood thirsty raptor - the island is never short of surprise ways for you to return to the lobby, that's for sure.

That's why you've got to have your loadout ready to best prepare you for any unexpected encounter. You know what they say: if you stay ready, you don't have to get ready.

You want to start optimising your loadout as soon as you touch down onto the island. Go for a 2:2:1 setup—two weapons, two heals, and one item of your choice. Opt for a mid range weapon like an Assault Rifle paired with a close-up option such as a Shotgun or Pistol. When it comes to heals, prioritise smaller items for quicker mid-fight recovery.

### TIP:
Need a mantra for duelling? Just remember: shoot, build, reposition, repeat!

# HIGH GROUND ADVANTAGE

In any form of combat, having the high ground is always a game-changer. If you can't get higher through natural terrain, then you've got to build up. If the space is too tight to really gain a significant height advantage, then keep moving/jumping and remember to aim downward as you go.

**TIP:**
Remember to keep your APM (actions per minute) up! Constant movement is unpredictable and makes tracking harder for enemies.

# PVE: HENCHMEN

Epic brought hostile AI to the island in Chapter 2, and PvE has been a staple ever since. Fighting AI shares some duelling tips with PvP, but there are additional factors to consider as well.

There's likely some form of henchmen on the island (you know, since there are always factions trying to tear apart the fabric of reality to take it over). They're usually stationed around POIs and are hostile, but they're no real challenge - their AI is pretty low level, so just jump and shoot downwards and it'll be over in no time.

# PVE: BOSSES

Bosses are way tougher, with significantly higher stats and better rewards for being able to take one down.

**TIP:**
Boss Characters rotate each season, so check online to see who you should be on the lookout for.

- Whenever you can, begin the fight from a distance with some headshots. Since most bosses have approximately 400 Shield and 100 HP, it's a solid strategy to kick things off.

- If henchmen decide to join the fray, be sure to switch focus and take them out swiftly. Ignoring them could lead to being overwhelmed by their numbers.

- Bosses appear just once per match, making them prime targets. Stay alert because other players can swoop in and take both you and the boss out at any time!

- Remember, the Storm can work in your favour. It's a risky strategy, but timing the fight during a shrinking circle could allow the Storm to chip away at the boss's health, especially if you've stocked up on healing items.

# VICTORY ROYALE MAZE

Can you make it from the Battle Bus to Victory Royale without meeting your end at the hands of the other islanders you meet on the way? Check out p.62-63 for answers!

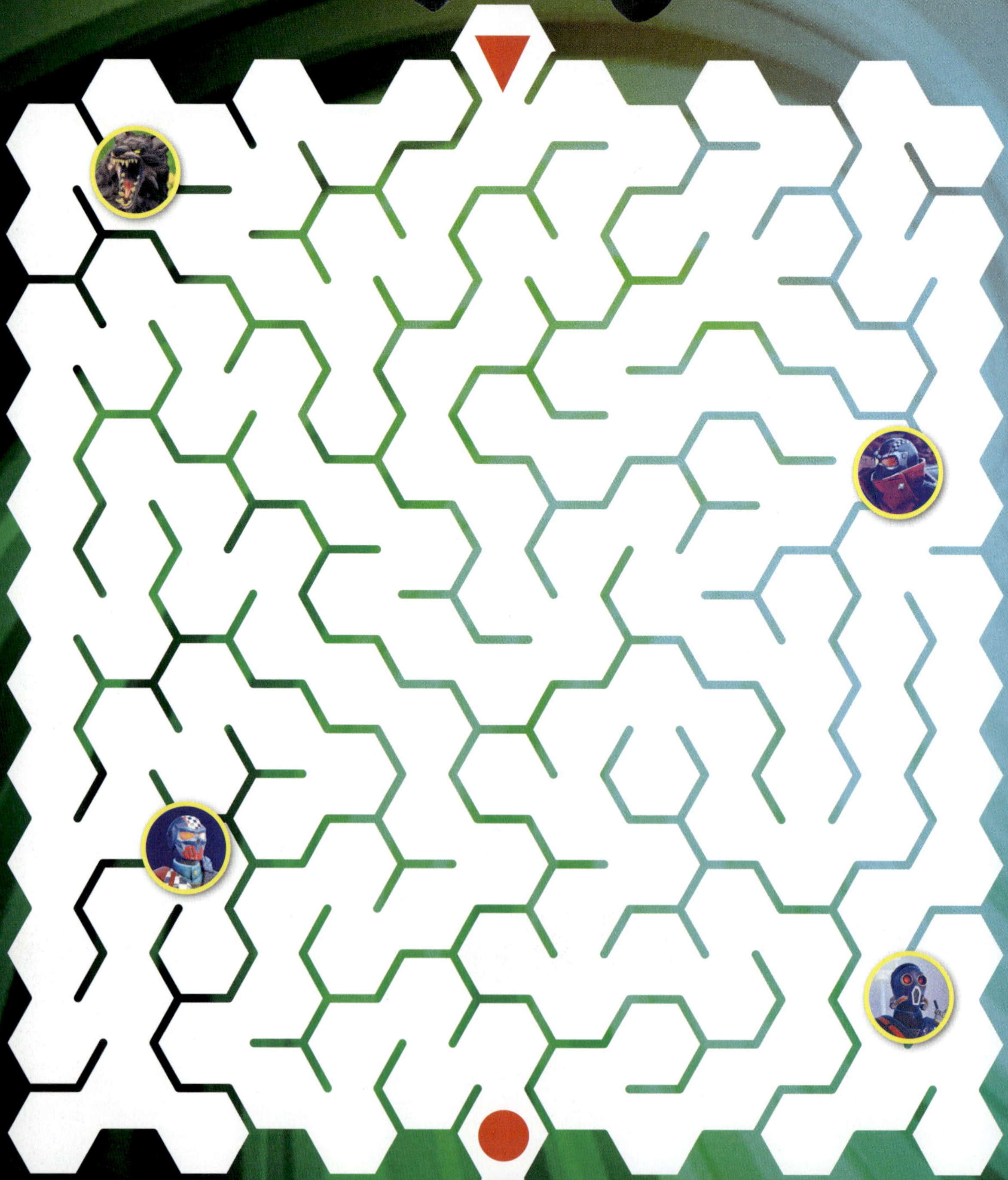

#1 VICTORY ROYALE

# ROLL OUT THE RED CARPET

Fortnite has long been the hottest spot for celebrities to pop up in - do you recognise some of the game's most famous faces? Check out p. 62-63 for answers.

1.

2.

3.

4.

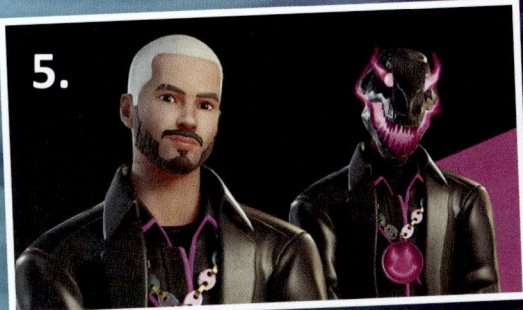

5.

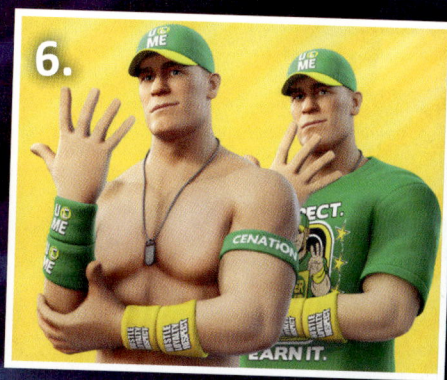

6.

# QUESTS

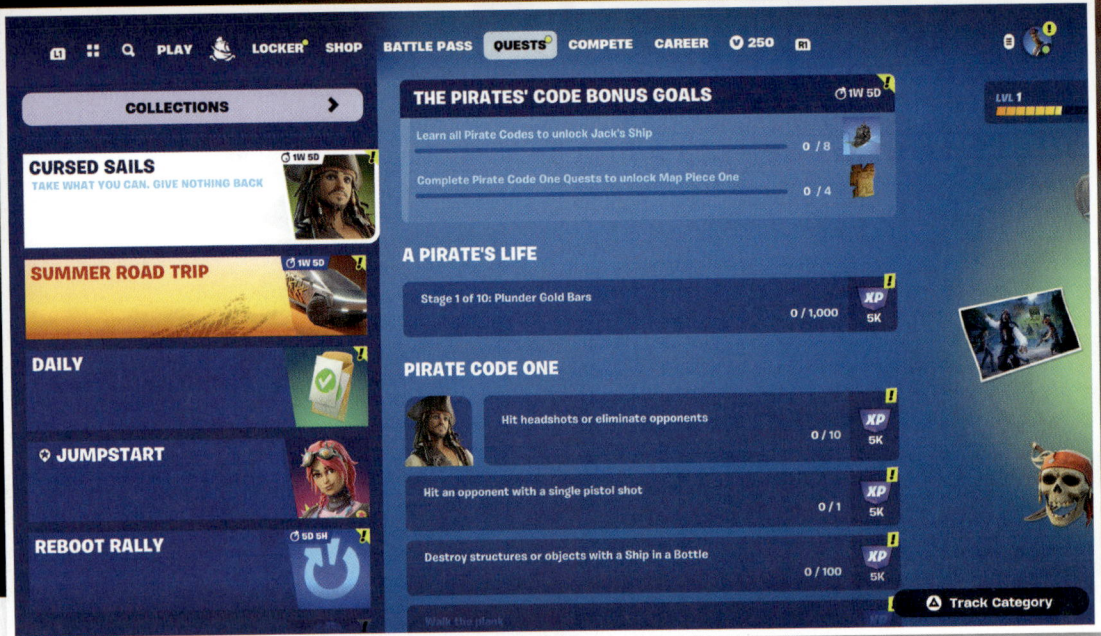

Ever feel like life needs a little bit more purpose than clicking heads? Well, cue the Quest system! Quests are a set of objectives for the player to achieve throughout gameplay. They can range in ask from modding a vehicle with a turret to thanking the bus driver. Reaching these gameplay goals will reward you with XP.

Like all things Fortnite, nothing is permanent, so the types of quest available can change at the drop of the hat (like Match Quests, we barely knew ye), but these are the main types that are usually live, or likely to return if they're benched.

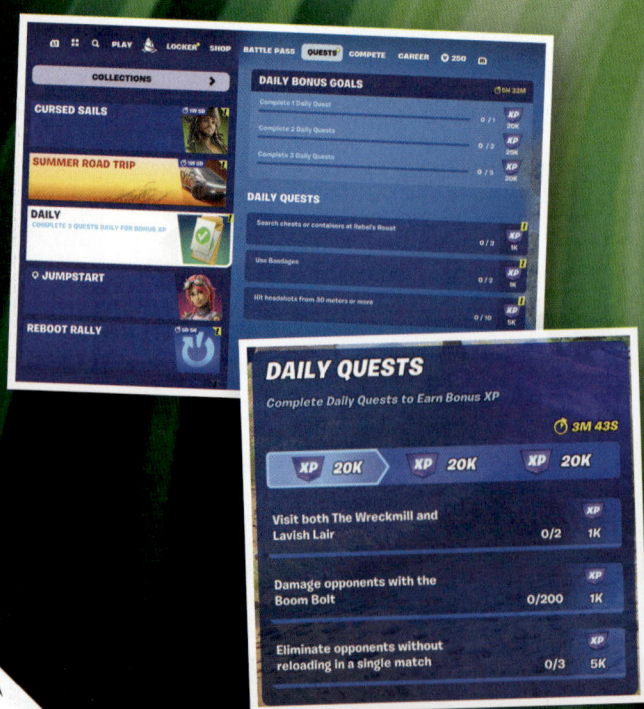

# DAILY QUESTS

Daily quests are designed to be achieved in 24 hours, so they're usually not asking for the world. Players are assigned three daily challenges at one time, with new quests becoming available to replace completed ones. They have little pay-off in terms of XP alone, but if you stack them enough to hit your daily bonus goals, you'll glean a lot more XP.

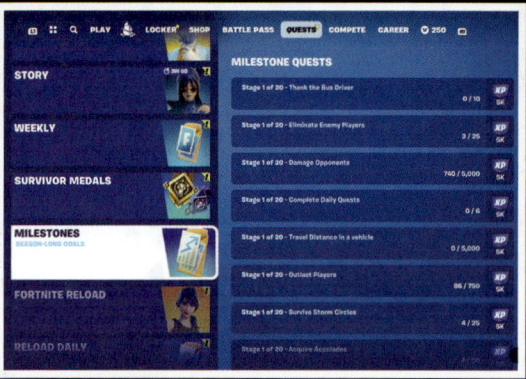

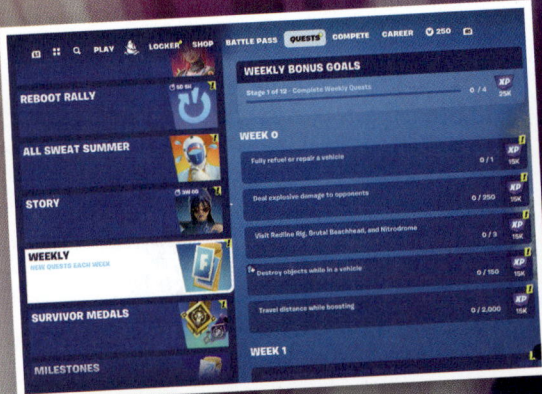

# MILESTONES

These quests are more about your experience with the game, rewarding you for all the big gameplay milestones you'll come across as you explore the island, learn more and play more. They're there to encourage players to try new mechanics (like when Augments first hit the scene) when they're introduced and make the most out of the Fortnite experience.

# WEEKLY QUESTS

Weekly quests are a bigger ask in terms of difficulty - usually going out of your way to complete one will be more of a risk to your survival during a match than a Daily would be. As such, the reward is much greater, as Weeklies typically grant around 15,000 XP per quest.

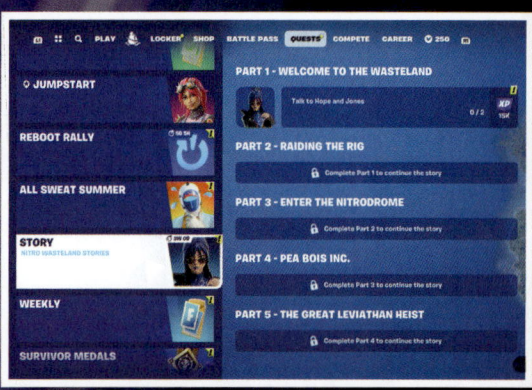

# STORY QUESTS

Honestly, we can't blame you if you don't know exactly what's supposed to be going down on that island. With time rifts, warring factions and sentient bananas, it can all be a little overwhelming to take in when you're also trying to save your own skin. Story Quests (also known as Snapshot Quests) are quests specifically dedicated to the in-game lore, leading you through the current season's bonkers narrative.

# WELCOME TO THE ISLAND

Behold, the battleground! Get ready to know every inch of this island like the back of your hand, because it's about to be the backdrop to all of your Battle Royale showdowns. Every great victor knows the lay of the land, moving about with ease and having one more advantage over the 99 other players vying for the top spot.

From iced-out mountain tops, tropical beach fronts, reality-ripping rifts and alien-infested trees - this island has seen more than its fair share of makeovers and iterations, but at its heart, it's always one thing: an arena!

# SPAWN ISLAND

Spawn Island is where the whole adventure really begins. This place has had just as many makeovers as the main island itself. It's situated near the main island, except in Chapter 4, where the Spawn Island was stationed in outer space.

In the first three Chapters of Fortnite, it was possible to return to Spawn Island during the Battle Royale match, either by building towards it and using a boosted vehicle for a final push, or flying a Choppa or flying saucer.

# LOOT ISLAND

Since Chapter 4, a little bonus island has been added to the main map. Loot Island is reachable only through a Rift, and features, well, a bunch of loot for you to plunder.

# ALWAYS ALLITERATE

Have you noticed that the majority of POIs on the map are alliterate (i.e. double consonants)? From the likes of Loot Lake and Retail Row from the early days to more recent additions like Ritzy Riviera and Fencing Fields, alliterate naming has been a longstanding location-naming tradition.

# IT'S ALIVE!

The island's capacity has totally levelled up beyond 100 players per match. Each island is alive and full of all sorts of creatures that are waiting for you to find them. Get the full scoop in Survival Guide: Wildlife chapter on p.28-29 and the Friends and Foes chapter on p. 30-31!

# BIOMES

The map may go through a bunch of changes, but they use a lot of the same biomes. Biomes determine what kind of wildlife and loot is likely to spawn in the area. The most common map biomes are:

- **Grasslands**
- **Farm**
- **Snow and Ice**
- **Beach**
- **Tropical Beach**
- **Rainforest**
- **Jungle**
- **Desert**
- **Woods**
- **Swamp**

# DON'T FORGET TO TIP THE DRIVER!

You know what they say about starting as you mean to go on? Well, it totally applies here. Your landing spot might seem like a small choice, but it could be the difference between an early elimination and snagging that Victory Royale. Choosing wisely means setting yourself up for success from the get-go, so don't sleep on it when you jump from that Battle Bus!

# WORKING OUT WHERE TO LAND

It's time to leap off of the Battle Bus! Now... where to choose... You have quite a few options when it comes to picking your landing spot. Don't forget to consider the following when making your choice:

- **Hot For Hot Drops?** They're named 'hot' for a reason - these are the most popular locations for players to land. Usually this is just whatever POI falls in line with the Battle

Hot drops usually have a ton of resources available, but the trade-off is early skirmishes and the risk of an early elimination. However, if you're trying to get a quick kill count, hot drops are a great spot to get a head start on that - just make sure you have an exit strategy ready if things go pear-shaped.

- **Don't Go Too Remote.** But don't go too far in the other direction, either. If you land in a spot that's too remote, you might be able

- **Keep it Balanced.** Landing is like finding the sweet spot between risk and safety. Hot drops? Total thrill, but risky business. Remote spots? Chill and safe, but not as rewarding. If you're after that middle ground, try landing a bit off the Battle Bus path, but still close to POIs.

# LAND → LOADOUT

No matter where you touch down, your top job is sorting out your gear. Whip out that pickaxe and get to harvesting mats, keep an eye out for potions and mushrooms to boost your shield, and snag your first set of weapons. If you dove into a hot drop, grab a shotgun for those close encounters. Opted for a quieter spot? Grab a rifle for those longer shots before you start trekking. Gear up right, and you're good to go!

# THE ART OF LANDING

Fortnite lets you experiment with a lot of the gameplay to discover whatever style you like the best, but there's really only one way to jump off of the Battle Bus and land on the island - the right way.

1. Aim Low. Landing consists of a skydive and a glide. Since the skydive is faster, you want to delay the glider's deployment for as long as possible. Aim for lower ground in order to maximise your dive time, then...

2. Aim High. When your glider finally deploys, scout out a high-ground for speedy landing and to get on your feet ASAP. This not only helps you understand the terrain and scope out your surroundings, but it also grants you an instant high-ground advantage against any players who landed nearby. Even if your drop zone lacks major elevation changes, remember: a rooftop beats the street every time!

**TIP:**
You can speed up your glider's descent a little by strafing left to right, or aiming your camera at the ground and pressing forward.

# PEELY CROSSWORD

How well do you know Fortnite's most potassium-rich pal? Can you solve the clues and fill in the Peely crossword below? Check out p. 62-63 for answers.

## ACROSS

**2.** The faction he joined in Chapter 3 (3,10)

**4.** His first time on the island as an NPC (7,1)

**6.** The rite of passage he went through to enter bananahood (8,6)

**7.** His role in his second faction (6)

**8.** His first faction (5)

**9.** His Chapter 5 kidnappers (3,7)

## DOWN

**1.** Peely's best friend (5)

**3.** His first location (3,5,5)

**5.** The name of his beach skin (7)

# EMOTE QUIZ

Everyone knows a Victory Royale isn't a Victory Royale without it being sealed by busting a move courtesy of an emote. There has been a countless amount added to the game's catalogue over the years, but let's be real - not all emotes are made equal. Can you identify some of Fortnite's most iconic emotes by the icon and a few letters? Check out p. 62-63 for answers.

1. _ R _ _ _ _ _ _   J _ _ _ _ _ _ _

2. G _ _   G _ _ _ _ Y

3. _ _ _ _ E T _ _   _

4. _ _ O _ _

5. F _ _ _ _ _

6. R _ _ _   _ _ _ M   _ H _ _ _

7. _ _ V _ _   G _ _ _ A

8. _ _ N _   _ A _ _

9. _ O _ _   _ _

# TREASURE RUN

Can you work out who's going to make it to the treasure chest first? Check out p. 62-63 for answers

# CHARACTER WORDSEARCH

Can you find the names of some of Fortnite's most iconic characters in the wordsearch below? Check out p. 62-63 for answers.

```
D  B  G  Z  J  X  M  A  C  Y  L  E  E  P  P  X  C  F  S  Y
A  Z  R  E  B  M  O  B  E  T  I  R  B  F  B  X  Q  R  A  U
V  E  A  N  I  T  S  U  R  C  D  H  F  G  Y  Y  J  W  D  M
M  E  L  L  E  B  A  Z  E  E  R  B  H  Y  T  R  U  F  I  P
E  N  O  B  K  C  A  B  L  C  H  I  A  R  A  T  L  L  M  R
O  A  S  G  N  U  C  K  A  R  L  B  O  V  W  R  E  L  Q  O
W  Q  F  S  E  C  Y  T  I  R  A  L  U  G  N  I  S  E  H  T
S  S  M  K  F  L  W  C  U  I  O  G  I  M  I  G  M  W  Z  I
C  E  L  Y  P  U  M  B  R  E  M  E  D  Y  U  G  N  V  R  S
L  A  H  P  S  U  L  Y  W  I  R  P  C  N  T  E  L  S  A  I
E  B  X  Y  D  O  B  A  E  P  W  W  O  Q  F  R  Q  K  S  V
S  H  Q  J  Z  E  R  I  M  A  R  B  B  X  R  F  Z  N  L  E
U  G  E  A  A  D  O  C  K  M  W  R  B  W  L  I  T  R  O  H
U  K  S  U  D  R  E  M  M  I  H  S  N  I  O  S  T  N  N  T
W  J  O  R  S  N  B  U  L  H  T  W  Y  O  P  H  D  B  E  N
I  K  A  A  E  L  M  H  M  H  P  S  Z  Y  I  K  R  C  N  I
P  C  F  N  L  Q  W  R  T  F  E  T  T  E  L  O  D  N  A  B
R  Z  I  J  E  F  J  K  V  N  Z  E  K  R  T  X  F  F  U  J
Y  I  U  V  M  M  K  O  X  B  K  V  B  V  L  V  T  V  U
O  H  R  B  B  R  Y  J  G  D  S  E  M  A  R  T  O  B  U  T
```

| | | |
|---|---|---|
| JONESY | BREEZABELLE | BRITEBOMBER |
| BANDOLETTE | SLONE | THEVISITOR |
| PEELY | CHIARA | MEOWSCLES |
| REMEDY | PEABODY | CRUSTINA |
| JULES | MIDAS | BACKBONE |
| TRIGGERFISH | RAMIREZ | SHIMMERDUSK |
| AURA | THESINGULARITY | |

# FACTION SCRAMBLE

The storyline of Fortnite has been... diverse, shall we say? There have been black holes, rifts, timelines and tears in the very fabric of the game's reality, and while their severity and consequences have been varied, they have largely been orchestrated by the story's different warring factions.

How closely have you been paying attention from chapter to chapter as to who's responsible for the island's current state? We've scrambled up the names (but kept the first of some of the game's most prominent factions and given their logos as a clue - can you identify them all? Check out p. 62-63 for answers.

1. TEH SNVEE _____

2. IEMGNDAI OERRD _____

3. TEH RNISEEASCT _____

4. OAHTNDOBU _____

5. SPEIR CTLU _____

6. TEH SOEYCTI _____

7. GOSHT _____

8. WRA ETFOFR _____

# SPOT THE DIFFERENCE

Can you spot all of the differences between these two Fortnite pics? There are 10 in total. Check out p. 62-63 for answers!

# PRO KNOWLEDGE CHECK

It's time to put your Fortnite knowledge to the test! How well will you score on this quiz on all things Fortnite? Check out p. 62-63 for answers.

## 1. WHAT'S THE MAX PLAYER COUNT FOR A MATCH OF BATTLE ROYALE?

a. 50

b. 100

c. 150

d. 200

ANSWER

## 2. WHAT'S THE IDEAL LOADOUT BALANCE?

a. 2:2:1 - 2 weapons, 2 heals, 1 dealer's choice

b. 2:2:1 - 2 heals, 2 dealer's choice, 1 weapon

c. 2:2:1 - 2 dealer's choice, 2 weapons, 1 heal

d. 2:2:2 - 2 weapons, 2 heals, 2 dealer's choice

ANSWER

## 3. WHAT SHOULD YOU KEEP HIGH IN ORDER TO MAKE YOUR MOVEMENT UNPREDICTABLE IN A DUEL?

a. BPM
b. CPM
c. XPM
d. APM

ANSWER

## 4. WHICH MAT HAS THE HIGHEST HP?

a. Wood
b. Cotton
c. Metal
d. Stone

ANSWER

## 5. WHICH BUILDING TECHNIQUE IS BEST FOR A SPEEDY ASCENSION?

a. Turtle
b. Ramp Rush
c. 1x1
d. Traps

ANSWER

## 6. WHICH FORAGED ITEM ALSO GIVES YOU A BONUS SPEED BOOST?

a. Apples
b. Cabbages
c. Peppers
d. Slurpshrooms

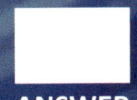

ANSWER

## 7. HOW MUCH DOES A PATCH UP SERVICE USUALLY COST?

a. 50 Gold
b. 100 Gold
c. 50 Shield
d. 50 XP

ANSWER

## 8. WHICH FISH ALSO HAS OFFENSIVE CAPABILITIES?

a. Spicy Fish
b. Slurpfish
c. Cuddle Fish
d. Jelly Fish

ANSWER

## 9. WHAT SPECIALIST NPC CAN HELP YOU WITH RESOURCES?

a. Heavy Specialist
b. Medic Specialist
c. Scout Specialist
d. Supply Specialist

ANSWER

## 10. WHICH WEAPON TYPE USES HEAVY AMMO?

a. Pistols
b. Sniper Rifles
c. Shotguns
d. SMGs

ANSWER

## 11. IF YOU DUEL AN NPC, WHAT TYPE OF WEAPON ARE YOU LIKELY TO RECEIVE?

a. Uncommon
b. Exotic
c. Mythic
d. Legendary

ANSWER

## 12. WHAT'S THE BEST WEAPON COMBO FOR AN SMG?

a. SMG + Pistol
b. SMG + Sniper Rifle
c. SMG + SMG
d. SMG + Explosive

ANSWER

# SHIELD SPLASH PUZZLE

It's squad healing time! Can you work out which Shield Potion the Shield Keg will fill up first? Check out p. 62-63 for answers.

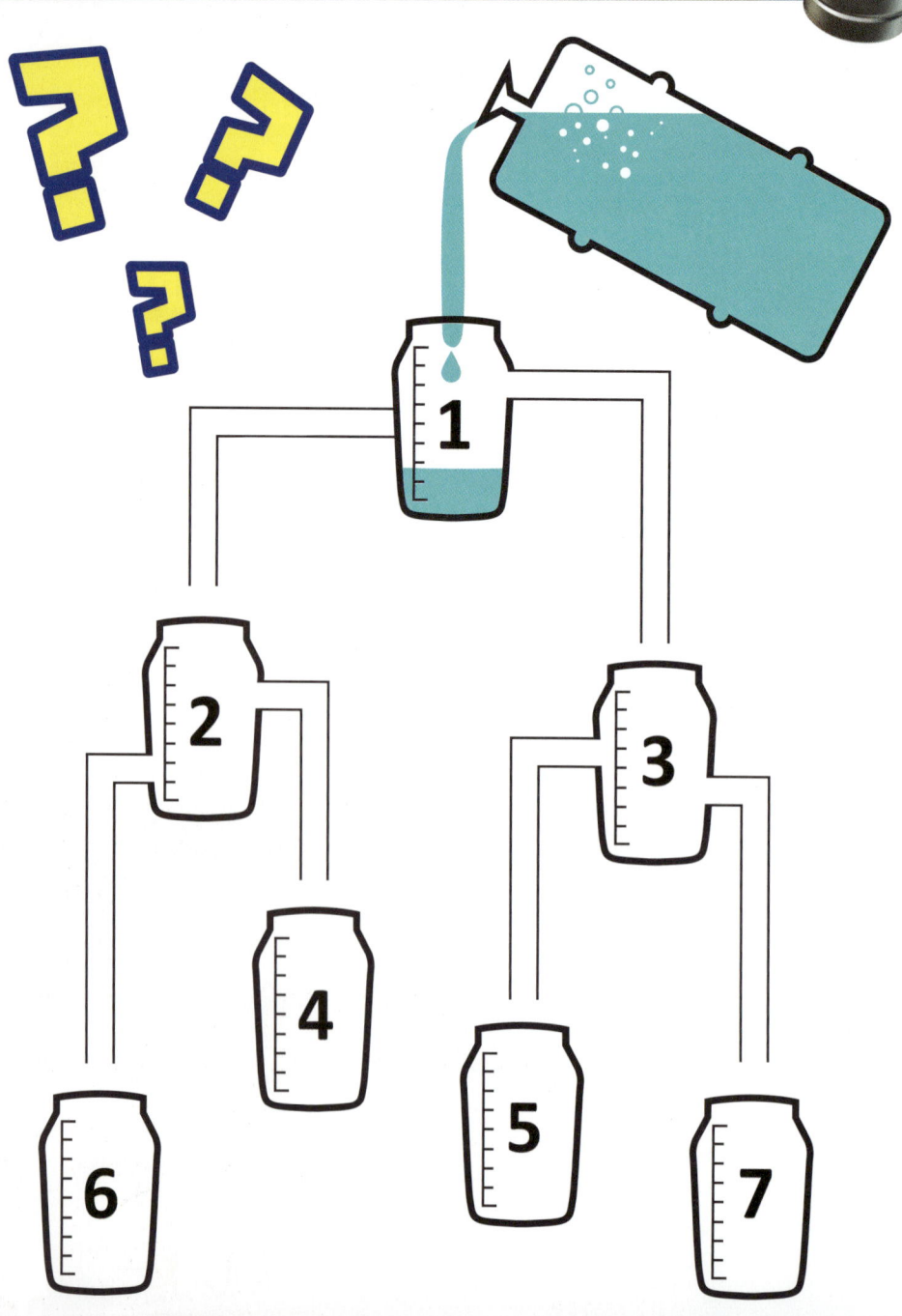

# GHOSTS OF ISLANDS PAST

We've come a long way since first touching down on Athena way back in Chapter 1. Changing islands (or in some cases, flipping) has become the main event for each new chapter, but that doesn't mean we've forgotten the battlegrounds of the yesteryears. Some locations are just too iconic to let go of... Can you remember which islands these legendary locations first appeared on? Check out p. 62-63 for answers.

1. Dusty Divot          _____

2. Retail Row           _____

3. Mount Olympus        _____

4. MEGA City            _____

5. Tilted Towers        _____

6. The Daily Bugle      _____

7. Lavish Lair          _____

8. Pleasant Park        _____

9. Reality Falls        _____

10. Rumble Ruins        _____

## TIP:

Psst! Here's a quick cheat sheet in case you can't remember the name of each island for each chapter:

- Chapter 1 - Athena
- Chapter 2 - Apollo
- Chapter 3 - Artemis
- Chapter 4 - Asteria
- Chapter 5 - Helios

# TLDR: PRO SURVIVAL TIPS

After diligently absorbing the last 60 or so pages of invaluable Fortnite knowledge and wisdom like a little sponge, here are some parting tips to give you the edge when it comes to surviving down on that rabid island.

## SETTINGS FOR SUCCESS

- Maximise your chances of survival by ensuring your settings work for you, not against you. First thing's first: make sure Turbo Build/Builder Pro is enabled.

- You might also want to consider toggling Autorun based on the context. Keep it off when you're in small spaces to minimise your noise output, but turn it on when you need to cover long distances quickly (it'll free up your fingers to check the map).

- Spend some time familiarising yourself with the settings menu. There are so many customisable options here that players often don't even realise are available. Every player is different, so a little tweak here and there to the default settings can make all the difference when it comes to how the game feels best to you. Find out what settings best

## LISTEN UP

- For the best experience, use headphones instead of relying on computer or TV speakers while playing Fortnite. The game's detailed sound design, like approaching footsteps, is more pronounced and immersive through headphones.

- Speaking of details, Fortnite has distinct audio cues for each weapon type. With practice, you can recognize these cues and anticipate which weapon an enemy is switching to, often before seeing the visual cue.

- Remember, your opponents are likely using headphones too, so they'll be listening just as attentively. Keep things quiet on your end by using stealthier tactics like crouch-walking when you're near enemies.

- Similarly, if you win a duel, there's a good chance your fight might have alerted nearby players to your location. Do a quick location scout before sifting through all of your kill-drop loot, and if it's late game, you might want to build cover around you before deciding what to keep and drop.

# STAY STEALTHY

- Sure, it's fun to be all guns blazing, but any pro will tell you the necessity of stealth when it comes to survival strategy. You don't have to be bush camping all match; it's just little things, like avoiding fully harvesting trees (leaving it partially intact can prevent the animation that could attract enemy attention) and always closing doors behind you (an open door is a dead giveaway that someone's inside).

- Stick to cover. Avoid crossing open areas unless absolutely necessary—you never know who might have a vantage point on you. Playing from cover gives you a strategic advantage, making it easier to plan your moves effectively.

# AND DON'T FORGET THE STORM!

- You know, amidst the chaos of Quests, Characters, other players and the occasional alien parasite, you'd be forgiven for forgetting that the Storm is still one of the biggest threats out there. Storm Sickness is a real danger, causing players who linger too long in the storm to take triple the damage.

- While outrunning the storm, stay alert! High chances are other players were also running into the safe zone, so expect more players around the edges of the eye. If you reach safety with enough time, you can take the opportunity to find cover and pick off any players trying to run back into the bubble.

# EXERCISE CAUTION

- A little caution didn't hurt anyone. In fact, it probably saved a lot of islanders, that's for sure. Again, it's not about playing a hiding game, but just staying wary of your surroundings. If you come across a lovely big pile of kill-drop loot, check it's not bait trying to lure you to distraction while someone else picks you off from nearby.

# QUIZ ANSWERS

## P42 VICTORY ROYALE MAZE

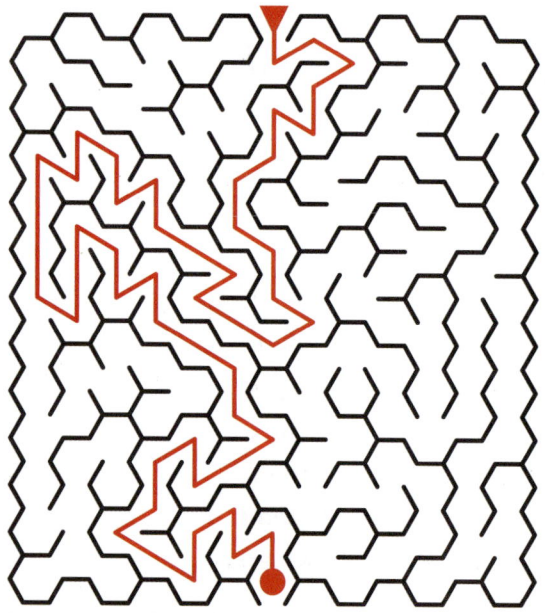

## P43 ROLL OUT THE RED CARPET

1. Lady Gaga

2. Billie Eilish

3. The Weeknd

4. Mr Beast

5. J Balvin

6. John Cena

## P50 PEELY CROSSWORD

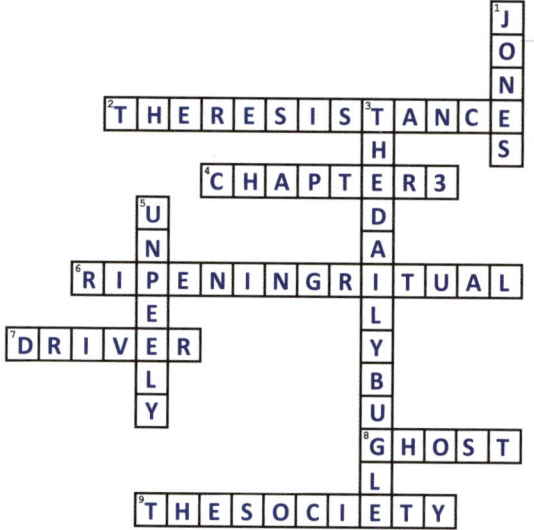

Across / Down answers:
- JONES
- THE RESISTANCE
- CHAPTER 3
- RIPENING RITUAL
- DRIVER
- GHOST
- THE SOCIETY
- UNPEELY
- THE DAILY BUGLE

## P57 EMOTE QUIZ

1. ORANGE JUSTICE
2. GET GRIDDY
3. TAKE THE L
4. FLOSS
5. FRESH
6. REAL SLIM SHADY
7. NEVER GONNA
8. NANA NANA
9. PONY UP

## P52 TREASURE RUN